rules & infatuations

Patrick Playter Hartigan

Double Movement Publications

ISBN: 978-0-615-24838-7

Design, production, and illustration by Patrick Playter Hartigan

Acknowledgments: Parts of this work appeared in *The Pacific Coast Review*

Cover Illustration: *You Move,* 2008, graphite stick and oil stick on paper, by Patrick Playter Hartigan

Double Movement Publications
Patrick Playter Hartigan
2239 SE 47th Avenue
Portland, Oregon, 97215

Contents

For Endi - and for John and Geoffrey, and afternoons over Hegel turned to evenings over beers at the Deadwood

1

Rockaway Visit

Look at the green all
this green the forest
is so green. Look how
green a forest can be

See the sky over seas
green and blue my eye
catches sky over seas
green or blue & green

Look at his face this
boy this look at this
face this man or look
at the trees the seas

Fausto Coppi from Heaven

It is simpler than they
said it should be. What
difference does it make
to you when I arrive or
when I leave; departure
quickens the blood flow
to your eyes. I see you
struggle with a bicycle
tire and shall remember
it as if it were my own
for longer than you can

Why do you pause in the
middle of things? Where
does it say pause? Life
isn't some circumstance
beyond our control. How
a child could love such
a woman or man is apart
from all understanding.

A woman closes a window
and opens a door to let
some more of the air in
--that was simpler (she
thinks) than imagining.
Everything is simple in
its doing yet should be
imagined. Don't I exist
imagining, constructing
swallows out of leaves?

All so simple - we sigh
from out of darkness. A
woman quickens her step
passing by, closing her
skirt against the wind.

2

No Ship Sail

Strict in this
in this poetry
in this lesson

in the lecture
toppling quiet

Strict in this
strict seeming
vertical scale

in conventions
spilling poems

A displacement
in conventions
One convention

Our revelation
reading others

A disappearing
form the truer
content vessel

A disappearing
poet truer yet

All day long a
box into a box
into another a

proliferation.
Notes to Notes

All night long
dreaming a box
dreaming poems

a machinery of
how I was here

Proliferations
names & rhythm
into a box the

disappearing &
cascading form

All day long I
imagine and do
you imagine we

will meet like
fallen leaves?

Garden Poem

Earth is a kind
of garden & you
are like a song
overheard there

I am with other
people you know
& we are within
another's reach

All day long an
orange sunset I
surprised while
hiding whittles

There a leaping
contingent vast
but not so vast
as to be dreamt

Painted hills I
am following my
promise to live
with us forever

Hail strikes at
our backs as if
the oceans were
vomiting pearls

What is simpler
than 1 2 3 What
can stop us any
more than 1 2 3

Earth is a kind
of number and I
am an invention
of my own there

Something in the rain...

suggests we have
something common
regarded or else

In a word flight
In a word firing
into their night

A population the
population hands
living to itself

I am this tender
ukulele resolved
a painted jungle

You are threaded
iron in a device
receiving breath

Here's a new day
& rain will fall
states something

The rounded keys
slip from a fist
& into that life

You carry within

Nursery Prospects

This one will tire us,
earth's seen her style
a million times before

This boy's a recoverer
a bouncer and a thief,
a dasher and a twirler

I espy a girl who sees
me first, her eye like
the desires of a storm

One boy forgets me and
chatters up against me
& smiling totters away

This girl stands still
as if earth might this
moment choose to break

Here are two who dream
as three for one is in
love with how he seems

There must be one that
will die if caught; we
will guess which it is

A girl leaves her seat
to present me with her
study: a tissue flower

A bus together we sing
for singing or doze we

pass old land together

A poem, JTH

Once there was a boy
Why was there a boy?
Once there was a boy
as easily as beeches
shiver the West Wind

Once there was a boy
Why was there a boy?
A question thrown as
a fence over prairie
muted and arose pure

Once there was a boy
Jackson Thoreau call
your father down, am
I closer to light or
darkness my only son

Friends Say

God tells us what is honest
and simple, just like that.

A reasoned creature doesn't
qualify itself; one fishing
craft alone is no indemnity
from loss occurring at home

On transplantation: subject
chases object; our rooftops
reflect moon light, as moon
casts the light it catches.

She comes through the field
unbroken by the grass...dip
goes branch and Twirl Swirl
says skirt I can twirl well

To and from nest and flurry
of wiped-out autumn dropped
dead & perfect dear here we
sit the egg upon merrily do

Earth shields itself w/leaf
and sky. We are like string
bayonets in a universe that
fears string No such animal

gives good milk. Nests made
along an avenue bright newt
heads popping about; quartz
tearing at each water drop.

Just like that our campfire
& in the morning make it go

Clear poem

What's clear? Most
things are clearly
some separate wish

Here is a fulcrum,
& in a day how fly
and princess marry

The transponding I
hooks its beams in
my goldenly garret

Up the street that
is the good street
leading up to Mary

And as I face this
thing I wish where
lives Mary amidst?

The numbered block
tumbles & scatters
underneath the bed

One, then three...
then 2...then zero
pigeons on a ledge

I am cautious am I
& you are cautious
too. A silver coin

fires the engines;
a silver stick can
set an engine free

Collectibles Away

What is original
when I see cloud
like a bad cloud

Distinguishables
disappear Shadow
steps forth glad

We all disappear
Fortunate couple
tottering across

plain America ca
before I gave up
How can a thing,

disappearing, be
so sure of loss,
punctuated, glad

Silk sleeves are
fluffed now Blue
eyeliner applied

Onto a Boulevard
where poets true
any poet will do

Sonnet 1

tired
horse
tired
lever

treed
horse
trees
above

issue
lemon
solid
drops

where
I can
tired
shout

Sonnet 2

You will on a given day bicycle
through my towns You will neglect
to mention to others that you are
happiest when left to yourself.

You fall, you fall in love, you
fall through the crack you choose
to fall through. What will become
of songs we sing while falling?

You will on a given day bicycle
to the waterfront. Women spinning
hoops of fire cannot compete with
a rose petal blown across town!

Sonnet 3

We will sing a song in French,
the beetle and the blue glass.

We are wakened to a bright sun
The beetle and the blue glass.

Father nods & rumples our hair
The beetle and the blue glass.

Chris too is heading to school
The beetle and the blue glass.

All day long my mind's humming
The beetle and the blue glass.

Children break their hearts at
school beetle & the blue glass

Dark is an intelligent whisper
The blue glass and the beetle.

Eclogue

God is in the bucket

seat, poised against
the underlying trash

One thousand islands
rattling in the fist
of a solitary player

You two come on out.
When the band really
heats up go offstage

You are guaranteed a
view that will go on
forever Talk it over

If only book by book
were learning, brick
by brick a good home

Nobody guarantees my
bees; no sufficiency
for blind guarantees

You have pleasures I
presume; but compare
the bran new bicycle

That time when young
men fly apart like a
wind-blown waterfall

Ocean Poem

Do you like me?
Does everything
fall into place

Are you like me
wondering at my
floating castle

floating castle
frozen clouds a
dark frozen sea

A child recalls
he is lost this
dark frozen sea

Lilies spring a
sheep grazes my
dark frozen sea

Are we distinct
in our drowning
in our drowning

floating castle
Are we alike Am
I simply happy?

How to share to
participate the
earth the poems

Are you like me
earth the poems
How do we share

All day long my
clock, abstract
lung, tick tock

A woman at hand
a woman and our
child tick tock

Frozen clouds a
meadow bright a
pasture pasture

blackberries or
similar berries
wend as I cycle

Frozen clouds a
cold front Come
solve and hail!

Only could they
limit this poem
will I dissolve

Never the thing
anymore but the
coming to being

floating castle
frozen clouds a
dark frozen sea

Child in hand I
place ourselves
against the sea

Sheet of silver
spray and sheet
of silver spray

Rest that night
No longer can I
dream the ocean

Are you like me
happily annoyed
at frozen sleep

What a solution
what a dilemma.
Never the thing

Nor an American
paradise laying
days in the sun

Are you like me
Silver bicycles
park under tree

Silver bicycles
vagrant pushing
a bicycle free:

All at one step
I am conscious.
All at one step

Floating castle
touch & quivers
at our doorstep

This day if day
is permitted to
begin; this day

a permission is
falling to land
in my heartbeat

Easy as a child
calling oceans,
easy as a child

Do you like me?
Floating castle
flip and scurry

Drift and hurry
The Dark Animal
tires of summer

Vagrant pushing
bicycle cartons
beneath bridges

Man and my form
Woman with poem
unsilent papers

inheriting form
Nothing beneath
vagrant bridges

Our inheritance
if facilitating
best survives a

lecture. coffee
pools while sun
shows what I do

I am exactly my
body and trails
of our body too

Everything will
change I change
everything must

Before a hill a
dark frozen sea
On this horizon

curled inwardly
ships ever fall
or never fallen

How then how do
we speak when I
do not know how

I do not know I
come to the sea
a child in hand

I leave the sea
a child in hand
Frozen clouds a

seagull buoying
overhead, grass
miles long bent

and broken with
watching oceans
gap and shatter

Where are we if
when writing we
are never here?

What exact land
profits thereby
can satisfy our

instant longing
What story will
suffice tonight

Nothing shatter
anymore Nothing
suffice tonight

Something ocean
Something child
Do you like me?

Floating castle
shadows cast my
dark frozen sea

A darker shadow
follows me this
close shadowing

Spilling form &
into the dirt &
into open seas.

3

French Press

The little boy stumbles
on an open can immersed
in the dirt of a nation
famous for rolling land

We sweep the earth with
garments entirely white
The singing and walking
thick with winter sleep

The boy says, Sometimes
the world is a stone...
and everything will one
day leave itself behind

www.ingramcontent.com/pod-product-compliance
Lightning Source LLC
Chambersburg PA
CBHW031335040426
42443CB00005B/353